Is Your Dog

A GOOD BOY?

POP PRESS

UK | USA | Canada | Ireland | Australia
India | New Zealand | South Africa

Pop Press is part of the Penguin Random House group of companies whose addresses can be found at global.penguinrandomhouse.com

Penguin Random House UK
One Embassy Gardens, 8 Viaduct Gardens, London SW11 7BW

penguin.co.uk
global.penguinrandomhouse.com

Penguin Random House UK

First published by Pop Press in 2025
1

Text by Poppy Del Rey and Mike Weedy

Typeset by Six Red Marbles UK, Thetford, Norfolk

Printed and bound in Great Britain by Clays Ltd, Elcograf S.p.A.

The authorised representative in the EEA is Penguin Random House Ireland, Morrison Chambers, 32 Nassau Street, Dublin D02 YH68

A CIP catalogue record for this book is available from the British Library

ISBN 9781529954425

Is Your Dog
A GOOD BOY?

THE ULTIMATE PAWSONALITY TEST

POP PRESS

Contents

'I wonder if other dogs think poodles are members of a weird religious cult.'

— Rita Rudner

‘My dog shows me the meaning of true companionship, beyond all the glamour.’

— Bradley Cooper

PART 1:

Introduction

This book will test whether your dog is a good dog.

Before we can ask 'is your dog good?', we must ask what is 'good'. Actually, no, before that we must enquire: what is 'a dog'?

What is a dog?

The dog is a descendant of the wolf. Dog evolution occurred as a result of wolves associating with human tribes. The bravest and most sociable wolves would hang around the tribes scavenging their refuse. These wolves would pass on their genes and the link between dogs and humans became ever stronger.

The domestic dog was then selectively bred by hunter-gatherers, or to give them their full title, hunter-dogbreeder-gatherers. Which is a bit of a mouthful and doesn't look great on LinkedIn.

When it came to hunting, dogs could help sniff out and attack prey for their human masters. When it came to gathering, one imagines the dogs were next to useless – 'Why are you bothering picking those berries, when we could be playing frisbeeeeeee?'

The difference between wolves and dogs:

- **Communication** – Wolves use their voices, faces and bodies to express themselves. Dogs make similar noises, but also use a lot of body language and puppy-dog eyes to communicate.
- **Problem solving** – Wolves tackle problems through trial and error, while dogs look to their human companions for help.
- **Maturity** – Dogs reach maturity at six to eight months of age whereas wolves do not mature until two to three years old.
- **Mimicry** – Dogs have no interest in impersonating grandmas.

The dictionary definition of a dog describes a *domesticated carnivorous mammal which typically has a long snout, an acute sense of smell and a barking, howling or whining voice.*

That could be a dog, then again it could be Ed Sheeran.

OK, let's break that down.

Dogs are defined as 'domesticated'. Well, my dog is domesticated in that she lives in a house (rent-free, I might add) but on the other hand she rarely volunteers to do the washing up.

'Carnivorous'? Yes, that checks out. Cassie loves eating meat . . . but she also loves eating newspapers.

'A long snout'? Well, I wouldn't want to say, I don't want to give her a complex. But . . . yes.

'An acute sense of smell'? It's hard to square with Cassie's keenness for sniffing other mutts' butts. But she doesn't get up each morning and spray Lynx Africa under her leg pits, so she clearly has a better sense of smell than teenage boys.

'A barking, howling or whining voice'?

People think if your pet barks it's a dog. Not necessarily: it could be a seal, a frog or even an owl. I haven't made that up, there's an owl in Australia that barks like a dog . . . the clue's in its name, it's called the 'barking owl' and it ain't from Dagenham.

But putting all that aside, if it looks like a dog, smells like a dog and barks like a dog, you're most likely in the company of a canine. And hopefully it's one of the good ones.

'Happiness is a warm puppy.'

— Charles M. Schulz

'Some of my best leading men have been dogs.'

— Elizabeth Taylor

What is good?

Roman Emperor Marcus Aurelius mused on what it is to be good: 'When you arise in the morning think what a privilege it is to be alive, to think, to enjoy, to love.' That sounds just like a dog. No hesitation, no regrets, just glad to be alive. Truly good dogs in the eyes of the emperor, living their best life. Mind you he also said, 'What we do now echoes in eternity,' and I'm sure dogs aren't thinking that when they're chewing the TV remote.

Plato divides good things into three classes: things good in themselves, things good both in themselves and for their consequences, and things good only for their consequences. So, if a dog destroys your lover's jumper that you hate, it is simultaneously a good dog and a bad dog.

That is why dogs do not make good philosophy students. They are too complex. Also, they would eat their own homework.

Like a dog about to settle down to sleep in his basket, we seem to be going around in circles here. Perhaps a more tangible way of considering whether dogs are 'good' is to consider what they do for others – and by others, I mean the important others. Humans.

'My fashion philosophy is, if you're not covered in dog hair, your life is empty.'

— Elayne Boosler

'When your children are teenagers, it's important to have a dog so that someone in the house is happy to see you.'

— Nora Ephron

What have dogs ever done for humans?

'Don't worry, Rex, you'll catch him next time!'

Hunting

Before the 2004 hunting ban, a certain breed of rural types thought foxhounds were 'very good boys'. Whereas foxes considered them a team of hired killers. One minute Chris the Fox might be enjoying a relaxing Sunday stroll through the delightful English countryside, the next he had fifty barking-mad killers triangulating his location. Poor Chris had never even played *Assassin's Creed.*

'This job's a relative breeze . . . last year I was herding cats.'

Herding

By minimising a dog's natural inclination to treat cattle and sheep as prey, farmers have selectively bred herding dogs to help them with their livestock. The Border Collie is the absolute don of bossing sheep about.

A farmer will consider his sheepdog a 'good dog' if they successfully marshal a flock of sheep. Whereas the sheep will be thinking, 'Don't try to tell me where I can and can't go, you yapping lunatic . . . you're such a farmer's pet . . . All right, all right, I'm moving, keep your fur on.'

'I had that Scott of the Antarctic in the back of my sleigh the other night.'

Pulling

Huskies are energetic, athletic and have a thick double coat which makes them brilliant at transporting humans across the Arctic tundra. They are happy to pull adventurers mile after mile in freezing conditions, which is of course great for anyone stranded in the North Pole who forgot to download Uber.

Dogs are also good for *pulling*, pulling. Y'know, how people got together before the internet. Pre-Bumble, the best way to find romance was to let your dog mosey up to another dog forcing a meeting with their owner. So a 'good' dog could lead to a great marriage. Although, equally, it could be the first step to a terrible divorce.

Protection

A good dog can keep bad people away from your house. An angry-sounding mutt will put off a potential opportunist burglar from raiding your homestead. What a good boy.

Then again, if your guard dog also has a tendency to chew antiques, wee up velvet curtains and knock over your bottles of Chateau Margaux onto your Persian carpets, is your good dog really any better than a bad burglar? If your guard dog is actually costing you money, you could try giving him the sack . . . but he'd probably just stick his head in it and knock even more stuff over.

Furthermore, your hot-headed hound may be an effective crime deterrent, but who else is he putting off approaching your front door? If Deliveroo drivers are boycotting your home, you'll be hangry and you'll consider your disturbed Dobermann a bad, bad dog.

The easiest way to spot a burglar is to observe whether they have a dog attached to their ankle.

Dogs are truly man's best friend – your human friends would never give you a lift home like this.

Companionship

Dogs are great for keeping you company – that's why they are known as man's best friend, right?

Except unlike a real best friend, they can't agree with you that your boss is an idiot or play video games or get a round in.

Then again, after you've had the most miserable day ever (i.e. a work day) with the most terrible people in the world (i.e. your work colleagues) and your pooch snuggles up with you on the sofa and lets out a sweet rumble of contentment, you know that your dog is your BFF and no human could ever hope to compare.

Now scientists have questioned whether a dog's companionship can enhance human physical well-being . . . but of course it does. Apart from anything, no goldfish is going to make you walk 10,000 steps a day.

Patient: 'I keep dreaming I'm walking down the street naked.'

Therapist: 'Hmm. Tell me about it.'

Therapy

The therapeutic talents of a dog can be overstated. To the best of our knowledge neither Sigmund Freud nor Carl Jung were Dachshunds. However, psychologists believe that the presence of a dog can have beneficial therapeutic effects, making humans calmer and less stressed.

Guide dogs

How can anyone say a dog who assists the partially sighted in living a full life is anything other than 'a good boy'? Read on, dear reader. A seeing-eye dog reportedly led four of his owners to their deaths in Germany in the early nineties. The hapless hound apparently directed his first owner in front of a bus, led the second off the end of a pier, pushed his third off a railway and walked his fourth into heavy traffic. The name of the wretched pooch – *Lucky*. You couldn't make it up. Unless a bored German journalist did.

Dogs also find it difficult to differentiate between red and green which is why very few pass their driving test.

'How do I know you're a real guide dog and not a Spaniel chancing his luck?'

'YOU SHOULD GET A DOG TO HELP YOU!'

Hearing dogs

Dogs have an acute sense of hearing – up to four times greater than that of humans, which explains why you'll never see a dog at a Rita Ora concert.

Hearing dogs for the deaf are less well known and celebrated than guide dogs for the blind. Hearing dogs will alert their hearing-impaired handler to important sounds like ringing telephones, doorbells, smoke alarms and alarm clocks. They are certainly good boys but probably quite resentful boys too as guide dogs get all the adoration, kudos and inheritances from old grannies.

'I'm not saying you're just making up numbers – I'm just saying I've never heard of a police cat!'

Police dogs

Police dogs are also known as K-9s. Their duties include sniffing out drugs, finding crime-scene evidence, locating missing people, protecting officers and attacking suspects. Which doesn't sound like it leaves much for the police officers to do. Let's hope their pay is on parity.

If you're a police officer, you'll believe a police dog is a 'good boy'. Whereas if you're a police dog you're probably only doing it to get your teeth into a cat burglar.

Military dogs

There are several sorts of military dogs that have assisted soldiers over the years. There are sniffer dogs (e.g. Springer Spaniels) that snuffle out bombs. There are mascot dogs (e.g. British Bulldogs) that help keep up the troops' morale. And there are attack dogs (e.g. Belgian Malinois) which . . . well they are not in the catering corps.

However, perhaps the dogs that are easiest to call 'good' whichever side of the fight you are on are mercy dogs. Mercy dogs (often Collies) would carry first aid supplies tied around their bodies and sniff out wounded soldiers on the battlefield. Not just good dogs but life-saver dogs. Mercy dogs, we salute you.

So, given everything dogs do for us you'd have to conclude that dogs are good.

'We're collecting for the war effort against c— . . .
Oh, sorry, wrong house.'

Dog behaviours

'I wonder if other dogs do that or if it's just me?'

Turning around before bed

There are a few theories behind this:

1. Many biologists believe wolves sleep with their noses to the wind so they could smell any enemies approaching. Their little circular dance lets them work out which way the wind is blowing.

2. It might also be a 'nesting' procedure which uncovers unwanted threats such as snakes. Which is somewhat overcautious if you are kipping in a basket in a semi in Tring.

3. Or maybe, by rearranging the bed area, they are indicating to other nearby wild dogs this particular spot is taken for the night.

These aren't really relevant to our modern dog's environment, but to them it's a hard-wired compulsive behaviour. Like us schlepping down to the kitchen three times before we go to bed to check we've turned the oven off.

'OK, I'm not owning up to that one. That is grim.'

Farting

Dogs – fun, friendly and, unfortunately, farty.

A dog will pass wind then after sniffing the air, look around in disgust as if to say, 'Who did that?' They will then leave the room, deeply disappointed in whoever did the deed. Sometimes dogs wake themselves up with the force of their own fart. Bonus points if they also leave the room.

Licking faces

All sentient beings need some form of expression. For humans it's the music of Beethoven, the paintings of the French Impressionists, the musings of the Romantic poets or 17th-century Italian mime. Dogs have licking. It may be linked to the comfort they felt when their mother licked them as a puppy in grooming.

So, when your dog is giving you a good licking it can mean they are happy to see you and wish to express caring through grooming. It is also thought that it can be a sign of submission to more senior members of the pack. But it's not only our faces that dogs lick. They also lick themselves *all over the place.* Dogs don't have bathrooms and if they did, they wouldn't have 'Now wash your tongue' signs. Maybe mum's spitty tissue wasn't so bad after all.

Your dog 3.4 seconds before trying to lick your face.

Eating grass

When we see our dog eating grass, it's easy to think this is more dog-based idiocy and stop them. However, dogs may eat grass for various health reasons, adding more fibre or vitamins to their diet to complement their dog food. Like a side order of naan. It could also be simply because they are bored – like when they chew on things around the house. Having said that, dogs will also eat string, shoes, cardboard, wood . . . I suppose these all have a lot of fibre as well. Are there a lot of vitamins in suede loafers?

After another unsuccessful hunt, Buddy would have to settle for a big mouthful of grass.

Be careful or your dog will dig right through your new kitchen flooring.

Digging

Like many dog behaviours, digging has several uses. Dogs may dig to catch small animals or to dig out prey. Sometimes it's done to shelter from the elements or make a cool dugout on hot days. A pregnant dog may dig to prepare a nest for puppies. In the garden we see them burying a bone or a toy to hide it from others.

It's also just something to do and get all that doggy energy out. Whatever the reason, they love digging. On the beach, in the garden, between the cushions on the sofa, in their bed, in your bed. Interrupt them and they'll stop for a moment, look at you, then go back to it with a new determination. Why do dogs dig? Because dogs dig digging. I think we've got to the bottom of that.

‘Dogs are my favourite role models.’

— Oprah Winfrey

‘If you get to thinking you’re a person of some influence, try ordering somebody else’s dog around.’

— Will Rogers

Traits

We will be judging your pooch on its greed, friendliness, discipline and intelligence.

A greedy dog (owner for scale).

Greed

Being a fussy eater is not inherently 'doggish'. If you offer a dog a lump of clay, will they make an exquisite vase? No, they will eat it. What do you think of this original Shakespeare manuscript? Can I eat it? Manolo Blahnik heels? Can I eat them? Pound of butter? Eat? Birthday cake with all the candles? Eat? You get the idea. But this is not the greed of a bad boy. No. It is a good dog being true to its nature. As long as we rein in these gastronomic tendencies with firm guidance and a padlock on the cupboards, we can enjoy our pooch's enthusiasm for all things edible and indeed inedible. Goood dog. Until we discover he's wolfed down the Sunday roast on Saturday. Baaad dog.

Friendliness

Good dogs are the ultimate social butterfly of the animal world. Everyone they meet is a potential best friend or a new fan club member and their idea of small talk is sniffing your pants then going straight in for a French kiss. Bad dogs are the complete opposite and become inexplicably furious when another dog has the audacity to go for a walk in their favourite part of the park.

'At least buy me dinner.'

Discipline

A well-trained dog is a disciplined dog and that is largely down to the owner. Consider the many ways dogs show good discipline – *Sit! Stay! Seek! Come!* And the ways they do not – ripping up sofas, defecating randomly, biting, drooling, leg humping, howling, eating birthday cakes, fridge raids, chasing pigeons. I'm sure each owner has their own list. We've seen pooches winning *Britain's Got Talent* for their precision dancing, so we know how disciplined they can be, which is an important point to remember when your pooch is stealing your baby's dinner. When all is said and done, if your dog isn't very disciplined it's probably your fault and not theirs.

Alfie loved to tell his owner off for not providing enough strokes.

Intelligence

The ideal dog can communicate when they want to go outside, remember hundreds of commands and even collect your slippers if your feet feel a bit cold, but there's a reason why one of the most famous dogs is called 'Goofy'. Any dog owner will have witnessed their dog doing one of the following this week: chasing their tails, digging madly, snapping at bubbles, fighting with shoes, walking into glass doors and of course getting incredibly excited about a leaf. It's a wonder they got the hang of breeding but then that sometimes gets a bit haphazard as well. Yup, dogs can be real idiots. As soon as you try any gardening, they will be digging holes everywhere and ripping up flowers you planted. 'Let's get all this rubbish out the way,' they're probably thinking. Let's not forget their contributions to getting dressed, doing laundry and untangling wires behind a desk. It's never quite the help we need but always delivered with a healthy dose of enthusiasm. Ironically, given the chance, a dog would gladly have a go at brain surgery.

'I'm a professor of string-of-sausages theory.'

‘You think dogs will not be in heaven? I tell you, they will be there long before any of us.’

— Anonymous, often credited to Robert Louis Stevenson

‘Dachshunds are ideal dogs for small children, as they are already stretched and pulled to such a length that the child cannot do much harm one way or the other.’

— Robert Benchley

PART 2:

The Questionnaire

Section 1: Intelligence – Is your dog daft or clever?

Question 1

My dog thinks bitcoin is what he did yesterday.

5	4	3	2	1
VERY MUCH SO	YES, I GUESS	NOT SURE	NOT REALLY	NO WAY!
❑	❑	❑	❑	❑

Question 2

My dog could only guard the house if the burglar was allergic to dog saliva.

5	4	3	2	1
VERY MUCH SO	YES, I GUESS	NOT SURE	NOT REALLY	NO WAY!
❑	❑	❑	❑	❑

Question 3

If my dog went on holiday, he'd spend the whole time sitting on the luggage carousel.

5	4	3	2	1
VERY MUCH SO	**YES, I GUESS**	**NOT SURE**	**NOT REALLY**	**NO WAY!**
❑	❑	❑	❑	❑

Question 4

I don't need a paper shredder,
I've already got a dog and a letterbox.

5	4	3	2	1
VERY MUCH SO	**YES, I GUESS**	**NOT SURE**	**NOT REALLY**	**NO WAY!**
❑	❑	❑	❑	❑

Question 5

When I point at something, my genius mutt just looks at my finger.

5	4	3	2	1
VERY MUCH SO	YES, I GUESS	NOT SURE	NOT REALLY	NO WAY!
❑	❑	❑	❑	❑

Question 6

If my dog was an emperor, his motto would be 'I came, I saw, I ran around in circles'.

5	4	3	2	1
VERY MUCH SO	YES, I GUESS	NOT SURE	NOT REALLY	NO WAY!
❑	❑	❑	❑	❑

Question 7

If my dog had a hat it would be one of those caps with a propellor on top.

5	4	3	2	1
VERY MUCH SO	YES, I GUESS	NOT SURE	NOT REALLY	NO WAY!
❑	❑	❑	❑	❑

Question 8

My dog truly believes in the invisible ball.

5	4	3	2	1
VERY MUCH SO	YES, I GUESS	NOT SURE	NOT REALLY	NO WAY!
❑	❑	❑	❑	❑

Question 9

If my dog was on *Mastermind*, their specialist subject would be walking into doors.

5	4	3	2	1
VERY MUCH SO	YES, I GUESS	NOT SURE	NOT REALLY	NO WAY!
❑	❑	❑	❑	❑

Question 10

My dog can't understand why they can't bring an enormous stick home with them every week.

5	4	3	2	1
VERY MUCH SO	YES, I GUESS	NOT SURE	NOT REALLY	NO WAY!
❑	❑	❑	❑	❑

'I let the dog out, or I let him in, and we talk some. I let him know I like him, and he lets me know he likes me.'

— Kurt Vonnegut

Section 2: Friendliness – Is your dog friendly or unsociable?

Question 11

My dog makes friends with pigeons, then acts offended when they fly away.

5	4	3	2	1
VERY MUCH SO	**YES, I GUESS**	**NOT SURE**	**NOT REALLY**	**NO WAY!**
❑	❑	❑	❑	❑

Question 12

This affable mutt licks the TV when other dogs appear on it.

5	4	3	2	1
VERY MUCH SO	**YES, I GUESS**	**NOT SURE**	**NOT REALLY**	**NO WAY!**
❑	❑	❑	❑	❑

Question 13

My dog has over a thousand followers on Instagram.

5	4	3	2	1
VERY MUCH SO	**YES, I GUESS**	**NOT SURE**	**NOT REALLY**	**NO WAY!**
❑	❑	❑	❑	❑

Question 14

If my dog worked in an office, they would always be offering to make tea.

5	4	3	2	1
VERY MUCH SO	**YES, I GUESS**	**NOT SURE**	**NOT REALLY**	**NO WAY!**
❑	❑	❑	❑	❑

Question 15

My dog can get over-friendly with the arm of the sofa.

5	4	3	2	1
VERY MUCH SO	YES, I GUESS	NOT SURE	NOT REALLY	NO WAY!
❑	❑	❑	❑	❑

Question 16

My dog would love to jump into the lion enclosure at the zoo for a game of 'chase me'.

5	4	3	2	1
VERY MUCH SO	YES, I GUESS	NOT SURE	NOT REALLY	NO WAY!
❑	❑	❑	❑	❑

Question 17

If my dog was a nightclub bouncer, he would let everyone in.

5	4	3	2	1
VERY MUCH SO	YES, I GUESS	NOT SURE	NOT REALLY	NO WAY!
❑	❑	❑	❑	❑

Question 18

At the Reading Festival, my dog would be the first down the mosh pit.

5	4	3	2	1
VERY MUCH SO	YES, I GUESS	NOT SURE	NOT REALLY	NO WAY!
❑	❑	❑	❑	❑

Question 19

My dog is thinking about getting a pet dog in order to meet more people.

5	4	3	2	1
VERY MUCH SO	**YES, I GUESS**	**NOT SURE**	**NOT REALLY**	**NO WAY!**
❑	❑	❑	❑	❑

Question 20

My dog would happily spare just two minutes to answer a corporate questionnaire . . . and tick the box for a follow-up call.

5	4	3	2	1
VERY MUCH SO	**YES, I GUESS**	**NOT SURE**	**NOT REALLY**	**NO WAY!**
❑	❑	❑	❑	❑

‘There ain’t a man livin’ who hasn’t talked to his dog.’

— Hank Williams

Section 3: Discipline – Is your dog wild or restrained?

Question 21

When I tell them to sit,
my dog thinks there's a silent 'h'.

5	4	3	2	1
VERY MUCH SO	**YES, I GUESS**	**NOT SURE**	**NOT REALLY**	**NO WAY!**
❑	❑	❑	❑	❑

Question 22

If you took my dog's coat off,
they would be covered in tattoos.

5	4	3	2	1
VERY MUCH SO	**YES, I GUESS**	**NOT SURE**	**NOT REALLY**	**NO WAY!**
❑	❑	❑	❑	❑

Question 23

When I tried to potty-train
my dog it sent me potty.

5	4	3	2	1
VERY MUCH SO	YES, I GUESS	NOT SURE	NOT REALLY	NO WAY!
❑	❑	❑	❑	❑

Question 24

When I say 'Gimme five!',
he thinks I mean five farts.

5	4	3	2	1
VERY MUCH SO	YES, I GUESS	NOT SURE	NOT REALLY	NO WAY!
❑	❑	❑	❑	❑

Question 25

My dog's idea of wild swimming
is to jump in the bath with me.

5	4	3	2	1
VERY MUCH SO	YES, I GUESS	NOT SURE	NOT REALLY	NO WAY!
❑	❑	❑	❑	❑

Question 26

When I tell my dog to 'let go',
he assumes we're playing tug of war.

5	4	3	2	1
VERY MUCH SO	YES, I GUESS	NOT SURE	NOT REALLY	NO WAY!
❑	❑	❑	❑	❑

Question 27

When I give him an order, their eyes say, 'You're not my real dad!'

5	4	3	2	1
VERY MUCH SO	YES, I GUESS	NOT SURE	NOT REALLY	NO WAY!
❑	❑	❑	❑	❑

Question 28

Given a chance, he'll pick a fight with the Hoover.

5	4	3	2	1
VERY MUCH SO	YES, I GUESS	NOT SURE	NOT REALLY	NO WAY!
❑	❑	❑	❑	❑

Question 29

The only trick my dog can do is magically make my kitchen towel disappear.

5	4	3	2	1
VERY MUCH SO	YES, I GUESS	NOT SURE	NOT REALLY	NO WAY!
❑	❑	❑	❑	❑

Question 30

My dog only barks if it's absolutely necessary. Like if they want to watch TV or they don't want to watch TV. Or if they want to check that they can still bark.

5	4	3	2	1
VERY MUCH SO	YES, I GUESS	NOT SURE	NOT REALLY	NO WAY!
❑	❑	❑	❑	❑

'The dog is a gentleman; I hope to go to his heaven, not man's.'

— Mark Twain

Section 4: Greed – Is your dog selfish or generous?

Question 31

My fingers become part of the treat when I offer my dog a snack.

5	4	3	2	1
VERY MUCH SO	YES, I GUESS	NOT SURE	NOT REALLY	NO WAY!
❑	❑	❑	❑	❑

Question 32

As far as my dog is concerned, every day is an episode of *Dog Vs Food*.

5	4	3	2	1
VERY MUCH SO	YES, I GUESS	NOT SURE	NOT REALLY	NO WAY!
❑	❑	❑	❑	❑

Question 33

My dog's idea of fine dining is going through the bins at the park.

5	4	3	2	1
VERY MUCH SO	YES, I GUESS	NOT SURE	NOT REALLY	NO WAY!
❑	❑	❑	❑	❑

Question 34

My biscuits dog has got a biscuits one-track biscuits mind. Biscuits.

5	4	3	2	1
VERY MUCH SO	YES, I GUESS	NOT SURE	NOT REALLY	NO WAY!
❑	❑	❑	❑	❑

Question 35

My dog thinks all meals
are a starter.

5	4	3	2	1
VERY MUCH SO	**YES, I GUESS**	**NOT SURE**	**NOT REALLY**	**NO WAY!**
❑	❑	❑	❑	❑

Question 36

If they see me reach for the tin opener,
my dog acts like they scored the winner
in the World Cup

5	4	3	2	1
VERY MUCH SO	**YES, I GUESS**	**NOT SURE**	**NOT REALLY**	**NO WAY!**
❑	❑	❑	❑	❑

Question 37

My dog is so greedy that when he was given a cone collar, he thought it was a food funnel.

5	4	3	2	1
VERY MUCH SO	YES, I GUESS	NOT SURE	NOT REALLY	NO WAY!
❑	❑	❑	❑	❑

Question 38

When I try to take my dog's bone away, they will see my arm as another bone to add to their collection.

5	4	3	2	1
VERY MUCH SO	YES, I GUESS	NOT SURE	NOT REALLY	NO WAY!
❑	❑	❑	❑	❑

Question 39

My dog will eat anything if you put gravy on it.

5	4	3	2	1
VERY MUCH SO	**YES, I GUESS**	**NOT SURE**	**NOT REALLY**	**NO WAY!**
❑	❑	❑	❑	❑

Question 40

My dog likes nothing more than food . . . as well as stones, grass, wood and gaffer tape.

5	4	3	2	1
VERY MUCH SO	**YES, I GUESS**	**NOT SURE**	**NOT REALLY**	**NO WAY!**
❑	❑	❑	❑	❑

‘Puppies are my favourite thing in the whole wide world.’

Ryan Reynolds

PART 3:

The Pawsonalities

That's it, you're done! Time to add up your scores and let's see what pawsonality your dog has.

Question 1–10

Intelligence score ____ Type D/C

A score of 30 or more makes your dog more daft than clever.

CLEVER **DAFT**

10 30 50

Question 11–20

Friendliness score ____ Type F/U

A score of 30 or more makes your dog more friendly than unsociable.

UNSOCIABLE **FRIENDLY**

10 30 50

Question 21–30

Discipline score ____ **Type W/R**

A score of 30 or more makes your dog more wild than restrained.

RESTRAINED **WILD**

10 30 50

Question 31–40

Greed score ____ **Type S/G**

A score of 30 or more makes your dog more selfish than generous.

GENEROUS **SELFISH**

10 30 50

Now you have your dog's score, we can place the four values together to make a pawsonality type.

For example: daft, unsociable, restrained and selfish, come together to make the type:

DURS.

On the opposite page we can see how these 16 types correspond to a different dog characters.

		DAFT		CLEVER	
		UNSOCIABLE	FRIENDLY	FRIENDLY	UNSOCIABLE
RESTRAINED	SELFISH	*Daft, Unsociable, Restrained, Selfish*	*Daft, Friendly, Restrained, Selfish*	*Clever, Friendly, Restrained, Selfish*	*Clever, Unsociable, Restrained, Selfish*
RESTRAINED	GENEROUS	*Daft, Unsociable, Restrained, Generous*	*Daft, Friendly, Restrained, Generous*	*Clever, Friendly, Restrained, Generous*	*Clever, Unsociable, Restrained, Generous*
WILD	GENEROUS	*Daft, Unsociable, Wild, Generous*	*Daft, Friendly, Wild, Generous*	*Clever, Friendly, Wild, Generous*	*Clever, Unsociable, Wild, Generous*
WILD	SELFISH	*Daft, Unsociable, Wild, Selfish*	*Daft, Friendly, Wild, Selfish*	*Clever, Friendly, Wild, Selfish*	*Clever, Unsociable, Wild, Selfish*

DURS *Bark Wahlberg* Page 86	**DFRS** *Paw McCartney* Page 88	**CFRS** *Mark Zuckerbowwow* Page 90	**CURS** *Elon 'DOGE' Musk* Page 92
DURG *Henry Chewdor* Page 94	**DFRG** *Roger Fetcherer* Page 96	**CFRG** *Albus Puppledore* Page 98	**CURG** *Barkimedes* Page 100
DUWG *Al Pupone* Page 102	**DFWG** *Christopher Walkies* Page 104	**CFWG** *Indiana Bones* Page 106	**CUWG** *At-tail-a the Hun* Page 108
DUWS *Pawcasso* Page 110	**DFWS** *Goldielicks* Page 112	**CFWS** *Kim Karda-chien* Page 114	**CUWS** *Droolius Caesar* Page 116

Bark Wahlberg

Personality type

Action movie star Bark Wahlberg is daft, unsociable, restrained and selfish. He's an action star and even used to rap! Yes, this hunky hero is a real bruiser who never backs down from a fight but somewhere buried deep is a heart of gold.

Behaviour to watch out for

This fella loves showing off his bulges and will fling himself headfirst into whatever adventure he can find.

Training tips

Be careful with training Bark Wahlberg – if you have seen *The Departed* you'll know that as well as being a dog, you might suspect that he is a rat!

Are they a good dog?

Everybody loves him and he's great with kids. Of course he's good!

Paw McCartney

Personality type

At 25% Beatle and 100% dog, this musical mutt is daft, friendly, restrained and selfish.

Behaviour to watch out for

Hugely energetic and graceful, this doggy dynamo loves dancing about and is never more at home than strutting their stuff down at the doggy park.

Training tips

Some dogs need treats and extensive training lessons to get them under control but with this dog all you need is love!

Are they a good dog?

Yes!

Mark Zuckerbowwow

Personality type

Mark Zuckerbowwow is clever, friendly, restrained and selfish. He comes over as a nice pooch but he's an absolute brainiac with the processing powers of a thousand laptops.

Behaviour to watch out for

Don't leave him alone with your phone as he'll give it a good chew and possibly harvest all your data.

Training tips

Don't let him get the better of you or he'll take over your life, then the world.

Are they a good dog?

Yes . . . there's no need to be afraid of his mega bites.

Elon 'DOGE' Musk

Personality type

Elon Husky is clever, unsociable, restrained and selfish. Elon is a shrewd little dude who can never have enough. Whether it's pats on the back or cold hard treats, Elon always wants more, more, MORE.

Behaviour to watch out for

Tell your neighbours to get used to a constant stream of puppies as Elon has already fathered a lot of pups. And he has terrible taste in friends – have you met Donald Terrier-Rump? If not, lucky you.

Training tips

Try to discourage him from barking at the moon. Or building a rocket.

Are they a good dog?

He's great and you don't have to charge him overnight.

Henry Chewdor

Personality type

As a former king of England, Henry Chewdor is daft, unsociable, restrained and generous. Part horrific brutal dictator, part loveable goofball.

Behaviour to watch out for

This guy can be terrifying and hold great power over all his subjects (doggy toys). He would love to make a furry winter hat out of a cat.

Training tips

Responds well to female attention!

Are they a good dog?

When he is not ruling you with an iron fist, yes.

Roger Fetcherer

Personality type

The great tennis player Roger Fetcherer is daft, friendly, restrained and generous. He'll also charm you with those puppy-dog eyes.

Behaviour to watch out for

This dog loves nothing better than playing with a tennis ball all day or jumping over a net, and he will certainly give you love. Although if he proves too much of a handful you might have to take him to the vet to calm him down – 'New balls please!'

Training tips

This is one who loves training and will devote himself to being the very best.

Are they a good dog?

One of the all-time greats.

Albus Puppledore

Personality type

As headmaster of Hogwarts, Puppledore is clever, friendly, restrained and generous.

He is as warm-hearted as a Midsummer's Day is long. This cute and canny canine makes every moment you spend with him seem magical.

Behaviour to watch out for

Your own. Careful you don't spend all your time with Puppledore because he's so loveable – and ignore everyone else in your life.

Training tips

I wouldn't try to teach him any tricks, he's already an absolute wizard.

Are they a good dog?

Yes, he's no Slytherin.

Barkimedes

Personality type

As a historic inventor, Barkimedes is clever, unsociable, restrained and generous. He's one of the most amazing dogs that has ever lived. When he's not chasing his own tail, he might be revolutionising irrigation systems in Ancient Greece!

Behaviour to watch out for

Archimedes approximated the value of Pi. Barkimedes works out the value of pie by eating it the moment you turn your back.

Training tips

This dog is far far cleverer than you, so don't even bother.

Are they a good dog?

We imagine that most dogs from ancient times would smell awful but Barkimedes is famous for jumping in and out of baths; so that sounds pretty good to us!

Al Pupone

Personality type

Al Pupone is daft, unsociable, wild and generous. Ooh, a real gangster dog. He's a criminal mastermind so you'd better stay on his good side.

Behaviour to watch out for

His namesake ruled an empire of crime in 1920's Chicago. Gambling, prostitution, chasing cats and scratching doors – you name it, he's into it. Don't be surprised if you find a sharp suit and a Tommy gun in his bed.

Training tips

It's hard to get this bad boy to do what you say. Any mention of Elliot Ness or the American taxman should get him into shape pretty quickly.

Are they a good dog?

Well, that's a bit tricky. If you are a fan of bootlegging, bribery, protection rackets, drug trafficking and murder then yes. You couldn't meet a gooder boy.

Christopher Walkies

Personality type

Oscar winning actor, Christopher Walkies is daft, friendly, wild and generous. Intense and strangely charming, this character has an infectious energy that will get you acting kooky too.

Behaviour to watch out for

This one is a real character who gets the attention of everyone in the room, whether he's barking and howling in his own unique way or tap dancing around with a watch up his backside.

Training tips

A dog like this craves stimulation and excitement so make sure you keep him busy.

Are they a good dog?

Yes, very strange but very good.

Indiana Bones

Personality type

Indiana Bones is clever, friendly, wild and generous. A loveable rogue who can charm his way out of almost any situation.

Behaviour to watch out for

Indiana Bones is a friendly, loveable dog that will steal anything that isn't firmly nailed down. Dogs like this thrive on a sense of adventure and love long walks in new places – as long as there aren't any snakes.

Training tips

Indiana responds well to treats, especially if there is a puzzle or challenge that he needs to overcome to earn his reward.

Are they a good dog?

One of the best! And he's whip smart.

At-tail-a the Hun

Personality type

At-tail-a the Hun is clever, unsociable, wild and generous. He is an indomitable spirit and the most feared dog on his patch.

Behaviour to watch out for

Just being an out-and-out psycho. Like walking around the front room with dirty paws. He's also very frisky and could be in the DNA of half of Europe's dogs within a few hundred years.

Training tips

Instead of asking him to play dead, maybe try to train him to stop attacking everyone.

Are they a good dog?

Yes he is . . . because I'm not going to tell him he's not.

Pawcasso

Personality type

Pawcasso is daft, unsociable, wild and selfish. He knows no restraint when it comes to expressing himself. Uncontrollable and controversial, yet maybe a crazy genius.

Behaviour to watch out for

In headstrong mode, a dog like this enjoys charging around causing absolute mayhem. This dog is irrepressible with a giant appetite for life. But be careful or he'll drive *you* as nuts as him.

Training tips

Good luck.

Are they a good dog?

The Andy Warhol of dogs – very good, very crazy.

Goldilicks

Personality type

Goldielicks is daft, friendly, wild and selfish. The defining characteristic of this four-legged friend is their insatiable appetite which gets them into trouble.

Behaviour to watch out for

Stealing other people's dinner and sleeping in their beds are favourite pastimes of this wayward mutt. Who knew a dog could get so excited about porridge? The lovely soft fur can be distractingly cute, causing you to forget she is essentially a greedy burglar.

Training tips

This dog has a strong food drive and will sleep anywhere, so can be motivated by treats or a blanket. She can be a bit wayward but unless you happen to live near bears who like eating porridge you shouldn't have a problem.

Are they a good dog?

For sure! As long as you're not a bear.

Kim Karda-chien

Personality type

Kim Karda-chien is clever, friendly, wild and selfish. She might come over as a bit dim but she's actually as sharp as a Rottweiler's tooth.

Behaviour to watch out for

Kim loves to cut a dasch and become the centre of attention. She's never happier than when you're taking her picture and posting it on social media.

Training tips

She's super-high maintenance. If you want her to do anything, it's going to cost you a lot in treats.

Are they a good dog?

She's a superstar.

Droolius Caesar

Personality type

Droolius Caesar is clever, unsociable, wild and selfish. Droolius is a dog that will mark his territory then mark the next-door neighbour's territory. Then the next. Then the next.

Behaviour to watch out for

Becoming a dictator or refusing to go to his bed. Droolius might appear to be a dribbling doofus but he's also a skilled scrapper.

Training tips

If he's in the mood for conquering the known world put him on a lead.

Are they a good dog?

Oh yes . . . unless you're a Bloodhound called Brutus.

Conclusion

So is your dog a good boy?

Of course. The evidence is incontrovertible. Dogs are always there to celebrate our accomplishments and help us survive the harder times with a friendly nuzzle and a concerned stare. Come what may, our most devoted friend stands by us and shares the trials and tribulations of our lives.

Yes, our trusty companions may be flawed, as are we all. Indeed, who among us can say they have never broken a diet for a treat, cried out in joy at an inappropriate moment or eaten their own vomit?

Picture the scene – you and your faithful hound stand at a dusty crossroads, the wind gently whistling across the desert as a lone bird squawks above. Your only possessions in a battered suitcase and for your dog an old neckerchief. You turn to them.

'Well, old friend. All the money's gone, the cupboards are bare, my pockets are empty and the landlord has kicked us out. So . . . It looks like we're walking.'

'Walkies! My favourite. Yay!'

Quote credits

Page vi from scoffpaper.com, 'Wooftastic Wisdom'; Page vii from petpress.net, 'Celebrity Quotes on Dogs and Happiness'; Page 6 from *Happiness is a Warm Puppy* (Cider Mill PR Book Pub LLC, 2006); Page 7 from *The Times*, 'A Challenge for Elizabeth Taylor' by John Higgins (1981); Page 10 from Elayneboosler.com/bio; Page 11 from Huff Post, 'Nora Ephron on Parenting' (2012); Page 42 from moderndogmagazine.com, 'Stars and their Dogs' (2025); Page 43 from American Foundation for the Blind, 'Learning the Basics with a Dog Guide' (2006): Page 53 from *The New York Times*, 'On Dogs, Especially Those Who Resemble Owners' (1978); Page 61 from *Slaughterhouse 5*, page 6 (Vintage, 1991); Page 67 from American Songwriter, 'The 16 Best Hank Williams Quotes' (2022); Page 73 from Mark Twain's letter to W.D. Howells, 2 April 1899; Page 79 from Buzzfeed Celeb, 'Ryan Reynolds and Robert McElhenney Play with Puppies While Answering Fan Questions'.

Image credits

Page 1 He made some hootch and tried it on the dog. A.B. Frost, Library of Congress Prints and Photographs Division Washington, D.C. 20540 USA http://hdl.loc.gov/loc.pnp/pp.print. Page 12 A dog chasing a heron off its nest in the reeds. Engraving by F. Place, ca. 1690, after F. Barlow. Wellcome Collection. Source: Wellcome Collection. Page 14 A shepherd's dog standing in front of a mountainous landscape populated by sheep. Etching by J. Scott after P. Reinagle. Wellcome Collection. Source: Wellcome Collection. Page 16 A man travelling on a sledge drawn by five dogs in Kamchatka. Engraving by S. Middiman, 1784, after J. Webber. Wellcome Collection. Source: Wellcome Collection. Page 19 A man in ragged clothes being bitten by a guard dog at the entrance to a town house; representing the sense of touch. Etching by T.L. Busby, ca. 1826. Wellcome Collection. Source: Wellcome Collection. Page 20 A rescue dog brings back a little boy on his back to a hospice. Line engraving. Wellcome Collection. Source: Wellcome Collection. Page 22 The dog Gelert guards the daughter of Prince Llewellyn after saving her from the attack of a wolf. Engraving by W.H. Mote after D. Maclise. Wellcome Collection. Source: Wellcome Collection. Page 25 A shoeless blind girl is led by a dog on a path. Sepia stipple engraving by T. Gaugain, 1785, after J. Northcote. Wellcome Collection. Source: Wellcome Collection. Page 26 A stockbroker feigning deafness to avoid paying the man who claims to have restored his hearing. Coloured etching, 1786. Wellcome Collection. Source: Wellcome Collection. Page 28 A dog with a heavy collar sitting outside a police station. Wood engraving by J. Knight after H. Weir, 1864. Wellcome Collection. Source: Wellcome Collection. Page 31 A cat and a dog facing each other on top of a ladder. Etching by J. Y. Carrington, 18--. Wellcome Collection. Source: Wellcome Collection. Page 32 A dog curled up and asleep under a tree. Etching by J.P. Le Bas after A.F. Desportes. Wellcome Collection. Source: Wellcome Collection. Page 34 Oil painting: a rabid dog by J. T. Nettleship. Wellcome Collection. Source: Wellcome Collection. Page 37 A dog retrieving a dead hare. Etching by J. Westley after G. Armfield. Wellcome Collection. Source: Wellcome Collection. Page 39 A hunting dog is chasing a duck in the water which escaped from his mouth. Etching by E. Hacker after R. Ansdell. Wellcome Collection. Source: Wellcome Collection. Page 40 Two dogs stare attentively at a hole in the haybarn's floorboards while another dog is watching the hay; vignettes show fairground attractions and humorous scenes. Etching by Frank Paton. Wellcome Collection. Source: Wellcome Collection. Page 44 St. Bernard Dog with mountainous background. Etching by T. Landseer after E.H. Landseer. Wellcome Collection. Source: Wellcome Collection. Page 47 A hare is bitten by a dog in its hind leg while another dog is growling at it. Etching by J. Griffier after F. Barlow. Wellcome Collection. Source: Wellcome Collection. Page 49 Dog caressing his master from Darwin's Expressions of Emotions. Wellcome Collection. Source: Wellcome Collection. Page 51 A dog in a buttoned waistcoat standing on its hind legs raising its paws. Etching by L.N. Lepic. Wellcome Collection. Source: Wellcome Collection. Page 55 Dog: You certainly have an advantage. Goat: Why so? Dog: Why, the summer showers don't take the curl out of your horns. E. Warde Blaisdell, Library of Congress Prints and Photographs Division Washington, D.C. 20540 USA http://hdl.loc.gov/loc.pnp/pp.print. Page 81 Head of a St. Bernard dog. Reproduction of an etching by F. Lüdecke. Wellcome Collection. Source: Wellcome Collection. Photography on pages 86–116 from iStock.